Build It Big

Focus: Designing, Making and Appraising

**PETER SLOAN &
SHERYL SLOAN**

In towns and cities people need places to live, work, and play. So offices, houses, churches, schools, and parks are built. Other things are built for the people who live in the towns and cities. Some of these things, such as bridges and dams, are very big.

Long ago, the Egyptians built
the pyramids. The pyramids
are some of the largest
buildings ever made.
They are made out of huge
stone blocks. Each pyramid
took thousands of workers
many years to build.

Some cities have very tall
buildings called skyscrapers.
The buildings rise up so high
they almost seem to touch
the sky. They take a long
time to plan and build.
The tallest skyscrapers are
more than 100 stories high.

Some towns and cities are built around rivers or harbors. Bridges are built so that people can cross over the water. The bridges must be very strong to support the weight of vehicles crossing.
Some bridges must be very long to cross wide rivers and harbors.

Walls are built across rivers to create dams. Dams are built to store water. The dam walls must be secure and solid to hold all the water. The water is piped to nearby cities and towns.

Many places have sport stadiums. The stadiums are built so that many people can watch a sports game and be close to the action. These buildings are often round in shape. Stadiums are built for sports such as football.

Amusement parks are built in many different places.
Rides are built inside the amusement parks. Disneyland is the most famous amusement park in the world. It has many interesting and exciting things to see and do.